Success With
Basic Concepts

New York • Toronto • London • Auckland • Sydney
Mexico City • New Delhi • Hong Kong • Buenos Aires

Teaching
Resources

State Standards Correlations

To find out how this book helps you meet your state's standards, log on to **www.scholastic.com/ssw**

Written by Danette Randolph
Cover design by Ka-Yeon Kim-Li
Interior illustrations by Janet Armbrust
Interior design by Quack & Company

ISBN-13 978-0-545-20093-6
ISBN-10 0-545-20093-8

Copyright © 2004, 2010 Scholastic Inc.
All rights reserved. Printed in the U.S.A.

4 5 6 7 8 9 10   40   17 16 15 14 13 12 11

Introduction

Parents and teachers alike will find this book to be a valuable learning tool. Children will enjoy completing a wide variety of activities that are both engaging and educational. The activities focus on basic concepts that will prepare children for kindergarten. These concepts include colors, shapes, number recognition, patterns, sequencing, alphabet recognition, and rhyming. Hidden pictures, coloring by numbers, dot-to-dots, and mazes are some of the fun activities used to engage children in learning about the concepts. Take a look at the Table of Contents and you will feel rewarded providing such a valuable resource for your children. Remember to praise children for their efforts and successes!

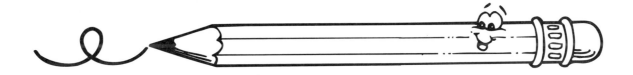

Table of Contents

Color Train

Draw a line to match each picture to the correct color.
Color.

Color Train

Draw a line to match each picture to the correct color.
Color.

Clowning Around

Color.

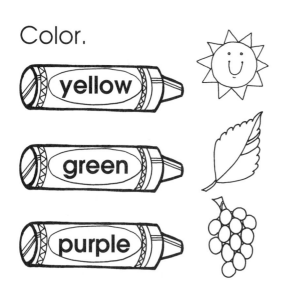

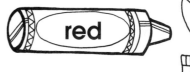

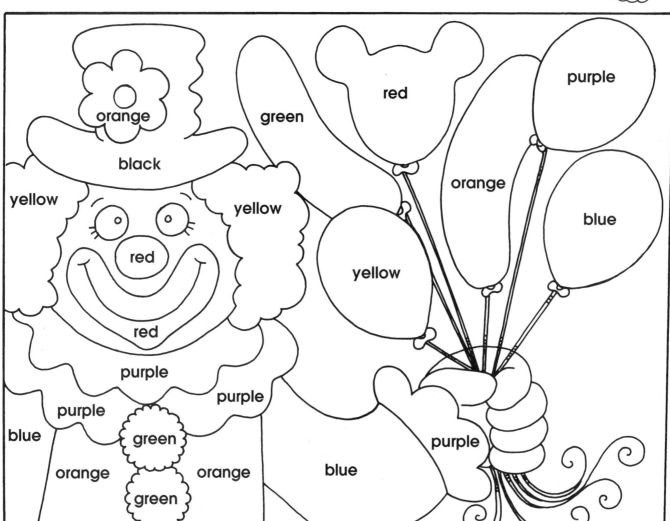

Rolling Through the Hills

Color.

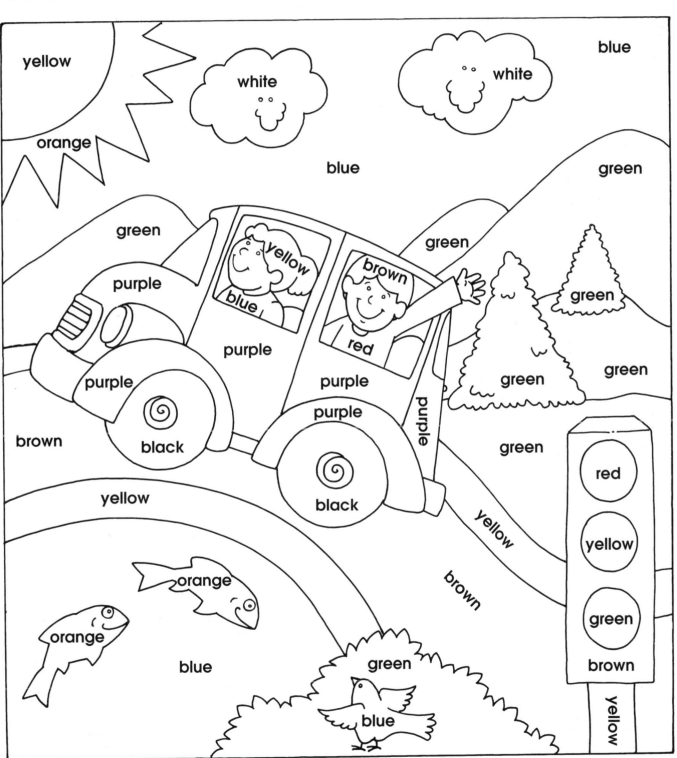

Name _____

Shape Match-Up

Trace each shape. Draw a line to match each object to its shape. Color.

square

circle

triangle

rectangle

Name _____

A Shapely Castle

Color.

 yellow ○  purple ◇  blue ▭

 green ▢  orange ⬭  red △

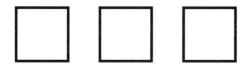

Shapely Sets

Draw a line to match each number to the set of shapes.

 one

 two

 three

 four

 five

Name _____

More Shapely Sets

Draw a line to match each number to the set of shapes.

 six

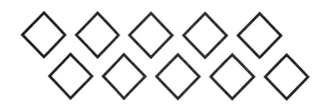

 seven

 eight

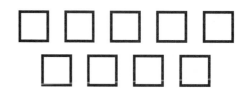

 nine

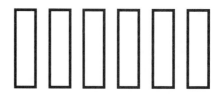

 ten

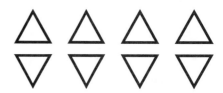

A Sea of Numbers

Color.

1 yellow 2 green 3 blue

4 black 5 red 6 brown

7 purple 8 orange

Crawl Before You Fly

Write the missing numbers.

Connect the dots from **1** to **10**.

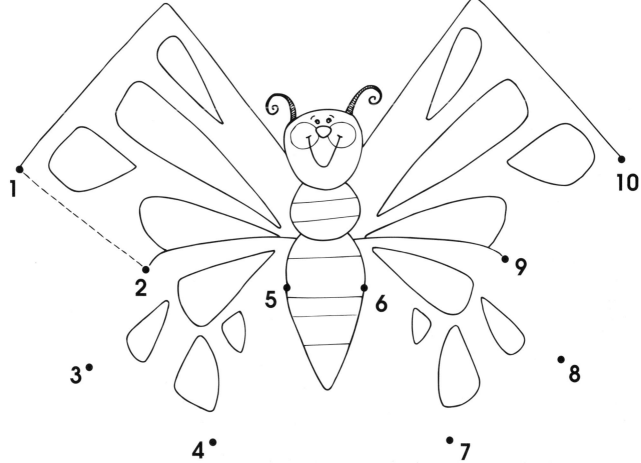

Counting Windows

Write the missing numbers.

123 Number Drive

Tricks for Treats

Count. Circle the dog with **less** bones.

Picking Flowers

Circle what comes next.

Name _____

What Comes Next?

Circle what comes next.

First Things First

Write 1 by what happened first.

Write 2 by what happened second.

Write 3 by what happened third.

Perfect Order

Write 1 by what happened first.

Write 2 by what happened second.

Write 3 by what happened third.

___1___   ___2___   ___3___

___1___   ___2___   ___3___

___2___   ___1___   ___3___

Name _____

Up on Top

Draw a ⚪ around the on the **top**.

Draw a ⚪ around the on the **top**.

Draw a ⚪ around the on the **bottom**.

Draw a ⚪ around the on the **bottom**.

In, Out, and All About

Color the animals that are **in** their houses.

Name _____

Above or Below . . . Sure You Know!

Draw a ☐ around the
above the .

Draw a ☐ around the
above the 🍃.

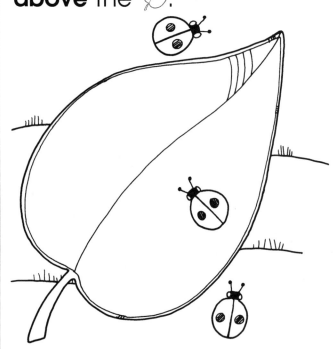

Draw a ☐ around the
below the .

Draw a ☐ around the
below the .

Name _____

Size It Up

Draw a ◇ around the picture that is **short**.

Draw a ◇ around the picture that is **long**.

Transportation Station

Draw a ☐ around the picture that is **big**.

 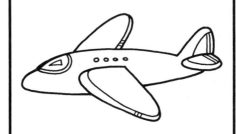 

Draw a ☐ around the picture that is **small**.

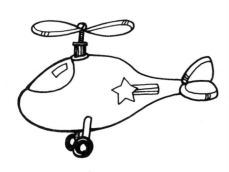  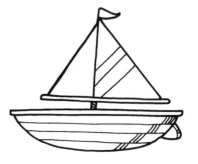

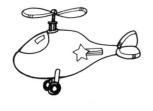  

Name _____

Mark the Map

Trace a ✋L or 🤚R path in each picture.

Triangle Teasers

Draw a △ around the picture that is **different**.

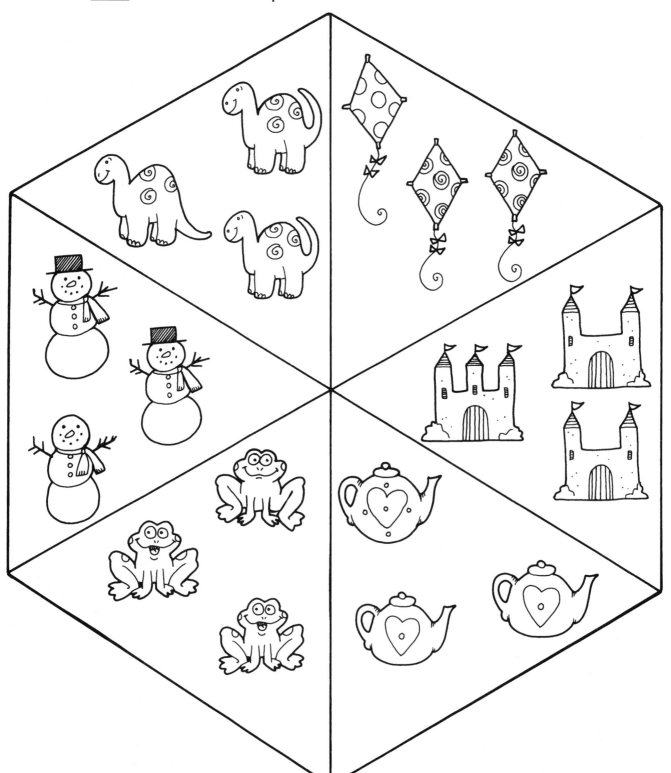

Side by Side

Draw a line to match the pictures that go together.

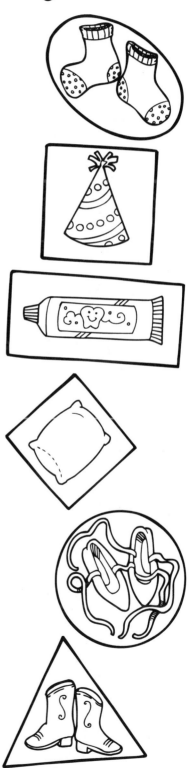

Together Is Better

Color the picture that goes with the first picture in each row.

Special Helpers

Draw a line to match the workers to their tools.

Out of Place

Put an **X** on the picture that does not belong.

Name _____

Rounding Up Opposites

Circle the picture that shows
the opposite.

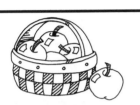

full

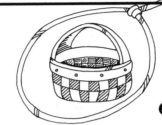

empty

loud

quiet

slow

fast

over

under

wet

dry

Name _____

Different As Can Be

Follow the maze to match the pictures that show the opposite.

Alphabet Parade

Name the picture. Trace the uppercase and lowercase
letter. Color.

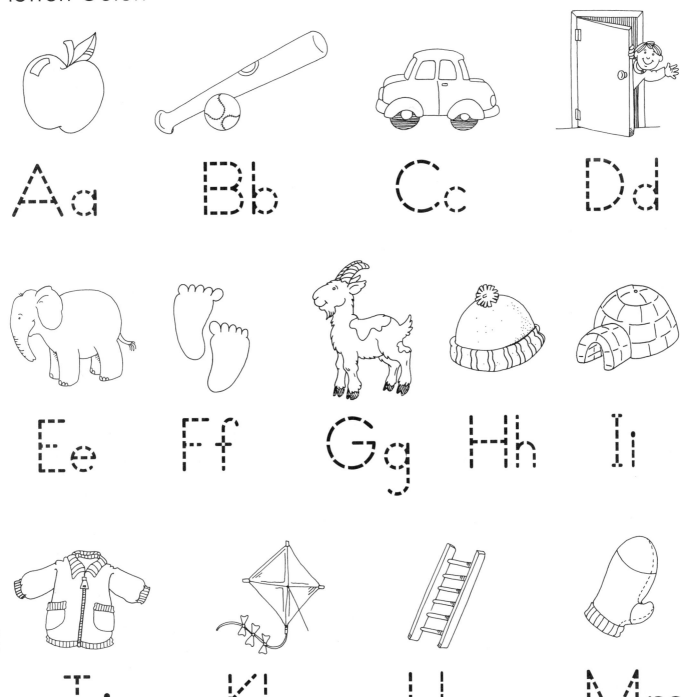

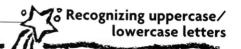
Alphabet Parade

Name the picture. Trace the uppercase and lowercase letter. Color.

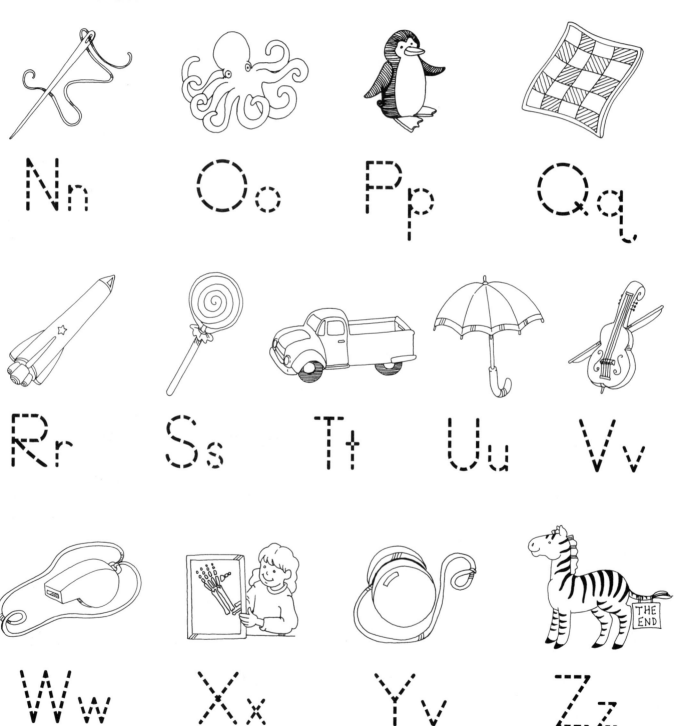

Nn   Oo   Pp   Qq

Rr   Ss   Tt   Uu   Vv

Ww   Xx   Yy   Zz

Name _____

Batter Up!

Write each missing letter.

Hop to It!

Color the lily pad with the letter that matches the frog in each row. Then circle the picture that begins with that letter.

A	D	A	E	(ant) (ladybug)
B	B	D	H	(car) (boat)
C	G	A	C	(crown) (flippers)
D	F	D	B	(book) (dog)
E	E	F	H	(egg) (donut)
F	C	E	F	(house) (fish)

Hop to It!

Color the lily pad with the letter that matches the frog in each row. Then circle the picture that begins with that letter.

Frog				Pictures
G	A	C	G	apple, grasshopper
H	H	G	B	hat, net
I	J	L	I	igloo, mouth
J	J	O	M	jar, monkey
K	L	I	K	lion, kangaroo
L	I	L	P	pear, lamp
M	M	N	K	monkey, key

Letter Flags

Color the carrot with the letter that matches the flag in each row. Then circle the picture that begins with that letter.

N (flag)	P	N	M	(igloo)	(necklace)
O (flag)	J	K	O	(jump rope)	(octopus)
P (flag)	O	P	N	(pizza)	(net)
Q (flag)	Q	U	X	(sun)	(quilt)
R (flag)	V	T	R	(yarn)	(ring)
S (flag)	S	Z	W	(snake)	(key)

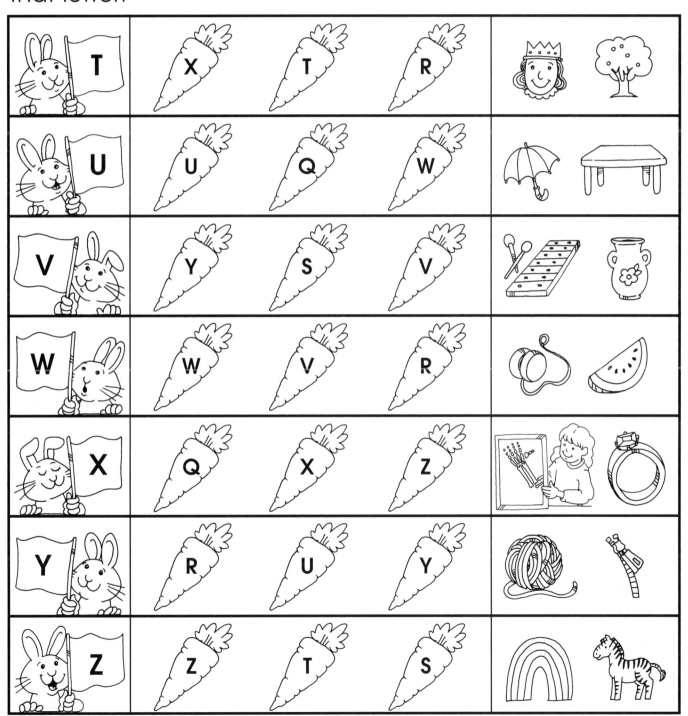

Name _____

Letter Flags

Color the carrot with the letter that matches the flag in each row. Then circle the picture that begins with that letter.

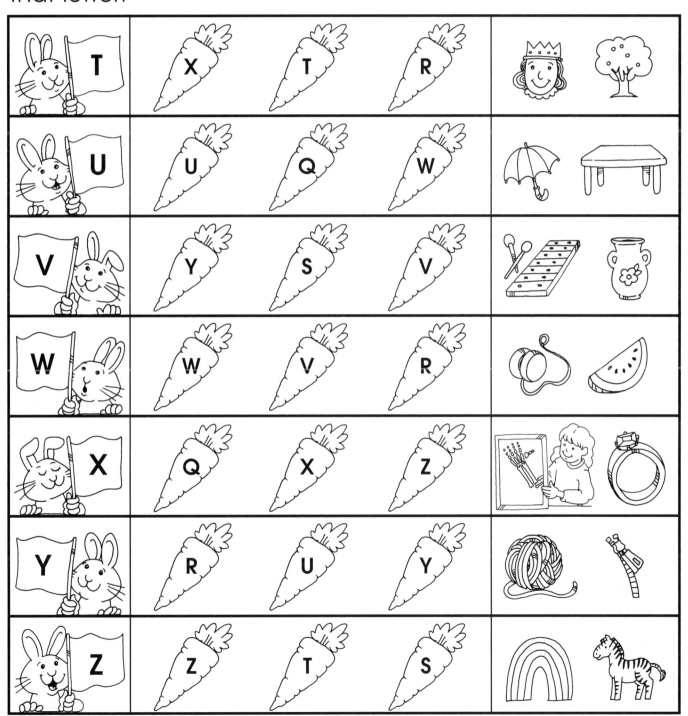

Out of This World

Connect the dots from **A** to **Z**.

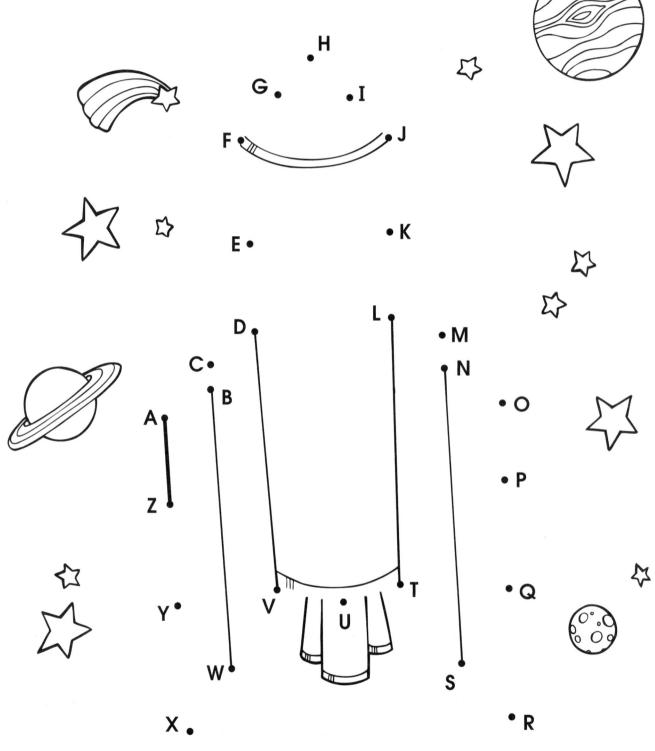

Play the Day Away

Connect the dots from **a** to **z**.

Connect the dots from **A** to **Z**.

Speedy Work

Name and trace the letters.

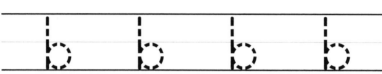

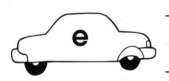

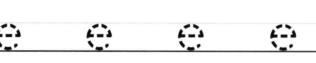

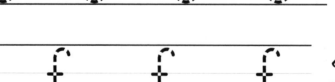

Mitten Matches

Name and trace the letters.

i	i	i	i	i	i
j	j	j	j	j	j
k	k	k	k	k	k
l	l	l	l	l	l
m	m	m	m	m	m
n	n	n	n	n	n
o	o	o	o	o	o

I
J
K
L
M
N
O

Letter Scoops

Name and trace the letters.

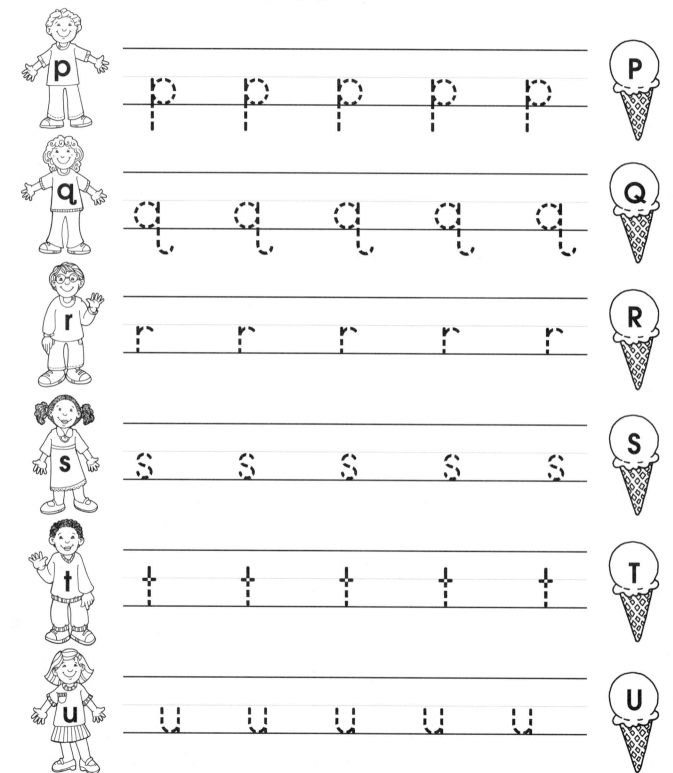

Name _____

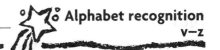 **Alphabet recognition**
v–z

King or Queen for a Day

Name and trace the letters.

Copyright © Scholastic Inc.

Scholastic Success With Basic Concepts 45

Time for Rhymes

Say the name of each picture. Circle the two pictures that rhyme in each group.

Check the Signs

Say the name of each picture. Circle the animal with the
picture that rhymes with the first picture in each row.

A Silly City

Circle 5 pretend things in the picture.